Contents

Foreword

Table tennis is one of the world's largest indoor participation sports. It is a full Olympic sport, and it can be played as a highly athletic and exciting competitive activity or as a relaxing and healthy recreation. It is truly a sport for all. Table tennis can be played by the young and old, by males and females, by the fit and not so fit, by the able bodied and those with disabilities. In fact, anyone can play and enjoy this great game.

Note Throughout the book players are referred to individually as 'he'. This should, of course, be taken to mean 'he or she' where appropriate.

Administration

The International Table Tennis Federation (ITTF), made up of member countries' national governing body associations, is responsible for the game's rules.

The European Table Tennis Union (ETTU) is responsible for competitive play in Europe.

The English Table Tennis Association (ETTA) is the governing body of the sport in England.

The English Schools Table Tennis Association (ESTTA) is an organisation backed by the ETTA, and is responsible for all school competitions.

The British Table Tennis Association for People with Disabilities (BTTAD) is another organisation backed by the ETTA, and is responsible for all training and competitions that are specifically organised for disabled players.

Further details of all of these associations can be obtained from:

The General Secretary
ETTA
Queensbury House
Havelock Road
Hastings
East Sussex
TN34 1HF

tel 01424 722525
fax 01424 422103

Acknowledgements
Text by Gail McCulloch, Chairman of the National Coaching Committee of the English Table Tennis Association. The publishers would like to thank Butterfly for their contribution to this book.
Photographs on pages 1, 19, 23 and 29 (left) courtesy of Sporting Pictures (UK) Ltd. Photographs on the front cover, pages 38 and 40, and the inside back cover courtesy of Eileen Langsley. All other photographs by John Wood.
Illustrations by 1–11 lineart.

Equipment

The table

Table tennis tables are 2.74 m × 1.525 m (9ft × 5ft), with a surface thickness of 22–25 mm (0.8–0.98 in).

The table stands 76 cm (2 ft 6 in) above the floor. Smaller mini-tables are available.

Tables are:

- standard – i.e. with two separate halves
- rollaway – i.e. the two halves are mounted on a central wheeled under-carriage for easy manoeuvrability
- rollaway with playback – i.e. a roll-away where one half may be vertical while the other half is horizontal. This allows for one player to practise alone.

▼ *Fig. 1 The table's dimensions and markings*

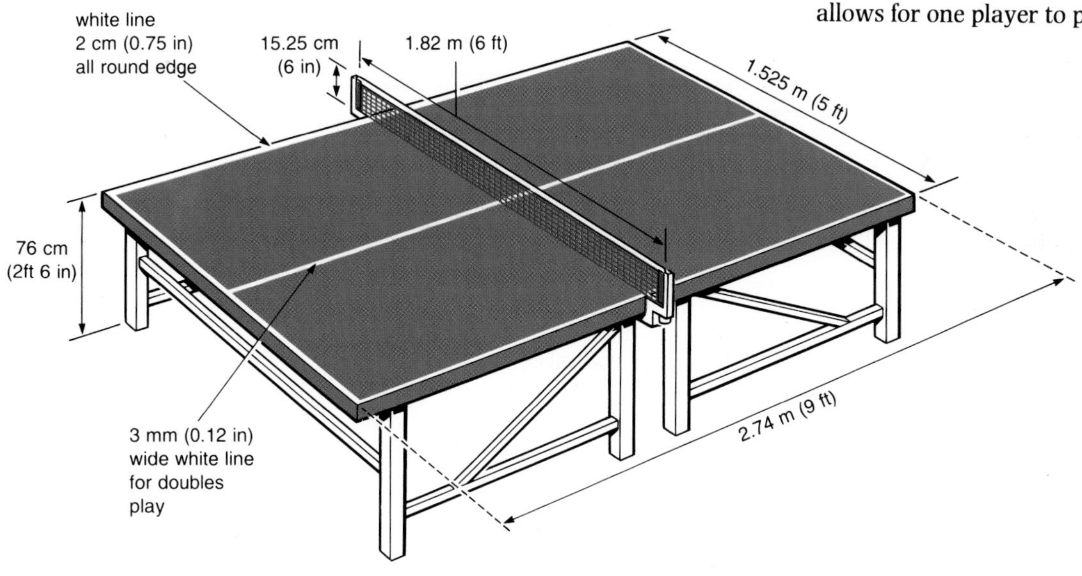

Tables are the most expensive item of equipment and should therefore be well cared for. Tables should be stored always 'face to face' to prevent the surface from being scratched. They should be stored on the central edge since damage to this edge will not affect play.

▲ *A mini table*

The net and posts

The top of the net is 15.25 cm (6 in) above the playing surface. The net posts clamp to the playing top so that the net is held firmly in place. The net usually has a cord through the top of it so that the tension can be adjusted. Most nets and posts are removeable from the table for easy storage.

▲ *Net and post*

The ball

Balls are made of celluloid or plastic, and are white, yellow or orange in colour. The ball is 37.2 mm–38.2 mm (1.46–1.5 in) in diameter and weighs 2.4–2.53 grams (0.08–0.09 oz). The quality of the ball is determined by a 'star' rating: the higher the rating, the higher the quality. All official competitions are played with three-star celluloid balls.

▲ *Ball*

The bat

Table tennis bats (or 'rackets') may be of any size, shape or weight. They are made of a wooden blade and normally two rubbers. (Penhold players (*see* page 8) may use a bat with rubber on only one side of the blade.)

The blades are made from several layers (or ply) of wood. The number of ply and the softness or hardness of the wood affects the speed and control of the blade. Greater speed generally means less control. Slow blades are made of three-ply soft wood, whereas very fast blades may be seven-ply with additional layers of carbon fibre.

The rubbers have a smooth side and a pimpled side. Most are used in conjunction with a layer of sponge which may be of varying thicknesses – 1.0–2.5 mm (0.04–0.1 in). The total thickness of the covering (rubber and sponge) on either side must not be more than 4 mm (0.16 in).

Rubbers are usually reversed pimples (smooth side out) but more advanced players may use anti-spin, short pimple or long pimple rubber, or a combination, i.e. two different rubbers.

Rubbers must be red on one side of the blade and black on the other side. In the case of a penhold player where only one sheet of rubber is used, the bat must still be red on one side and black on the other. This is usually achieved by staining the blade.

The beginner should choose a five-ply all-round bat with 1.5 mm (0.06 in) rubbers. This will give good control and reasonable spin.

▲ *Bats*

Clothing

Table tennis is a fast, athletic game and clothing should be comfortable and should not restrict movement. Short-sleeved shirts and shorts are normally worn. Clothing should be sweat-absorbent and of a colour that is not the same as the ball. Socks may be of any colour but are usually white.

Playing shoes should have a good grip but must be light and flexible for the fast movements that are required. The shoes should support the heel and instep.

Lighting

Local conditions will vary considerably, but good even lighting is a priority in table tennis. Tungsten halogen lights give the best lighting. Ideally, lights should be about 4 m (13 ft) from the floor.

Spin

Table tennis is often said to be a game of touch. This is true, but it is also a game of spin.

The ball is generally struck with either 'topspin' or 'backspin'. In addition, 'sidespin' may be added. If there is little or no spin on the ball, it is referred to as 'float'.

Topspin

Topspin is produced by starting the stroke *below* and/or behind the ball and contacting the ball as lightly as possible, i.e. brushing the ball in an upward and forward motion.

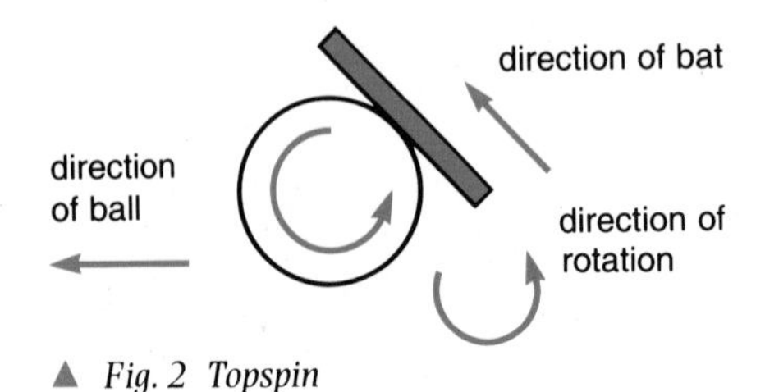

▲ *Fig. 2 Topspin*

Backspin

Backspin is produced by starting the stroke *above* and/or behind the ball and contacting the ball as lightly as possible, i.e. brushing the ball in a downward and/or forward motion.

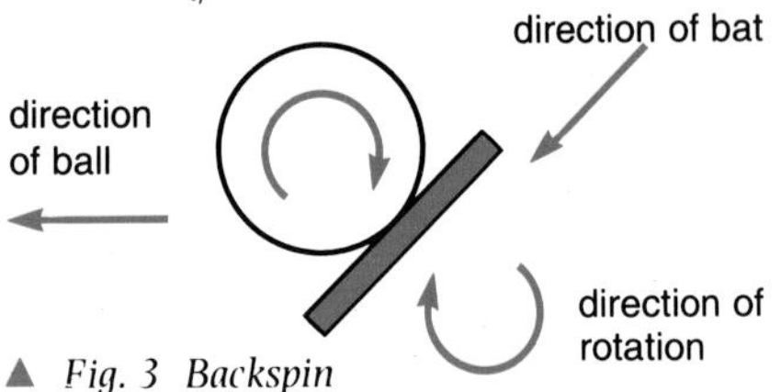

▲ *Fig. 3 Backspin*

Sidespin

Sidespin is produced by brushing across the ball lightly. This spin can be imparted in addition to topspin or backspin.

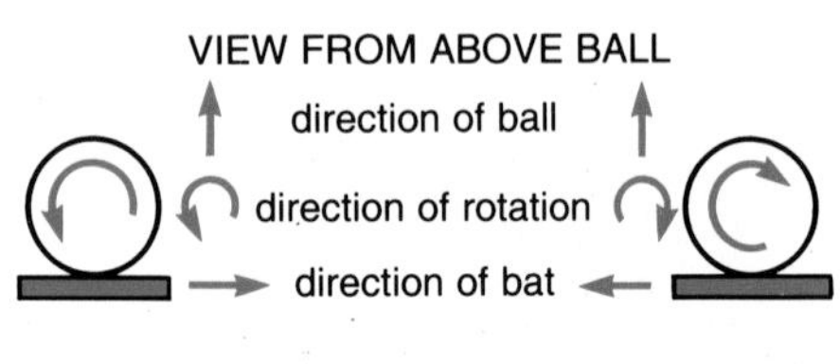

▲ *Fig. 4 Sidespin*

The effect of spin

The use of excessive spin is particularly effective on the serve.

▼ *Fig. 5 The effect of spin*

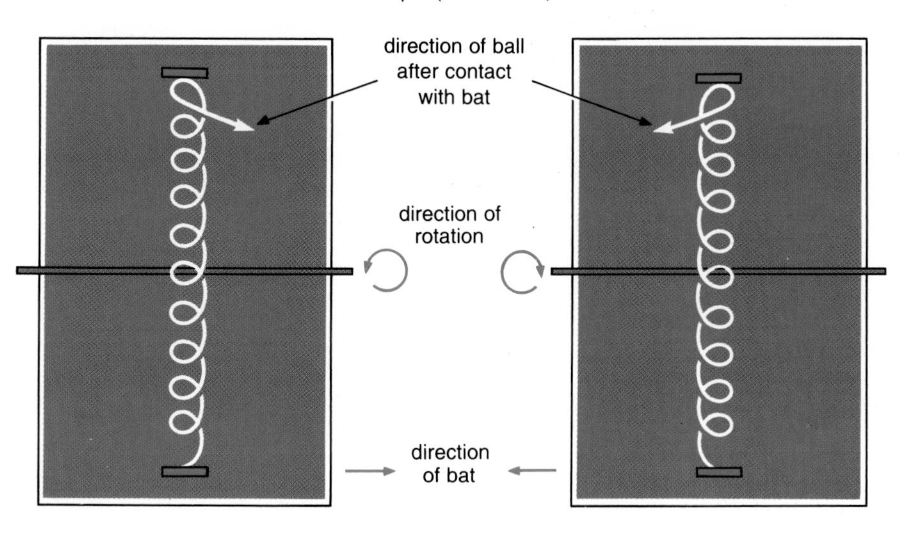

The grip

Most players use the 'shake-hands' grip where the bat is held in the palm of the hand and the thumb and first finger lie roughly parallel to the straight edge of the rubber. The other three fingers are wrapped around the handle to provide bat stability.

▲ *Forehand shake-hands grip*

▲ *Backhand shake-hands grip*

The 'penhold' grip is favoured by many Oriental players, but it has obvious restrictions since only one side of the blade is used.

Penhold grip, Chinese style ▶

▲ *Penhold grip, Japanese style*

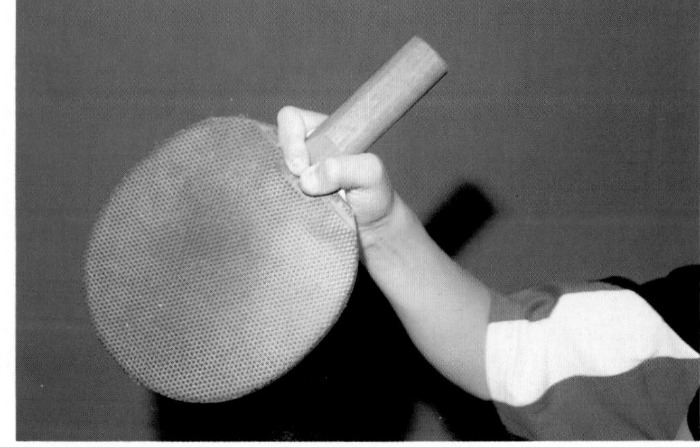

▲ *Penhold grip*

The ready position

At the start of every rally the player takes up a position that allows him to move quickly in any direction and to cover any angle that his opponent may choose to play to. The knees should be bent with the weight forward and balanced. The bat is held above the height of the table.

▲ *The ready position*

Bat angles

When hitting the ball, the bat angle is referred to as 'open' or 'closed'. An 'open' angle allows backspin to be imparted on the ball, whereas a 'closed' angle is needed for topspin.

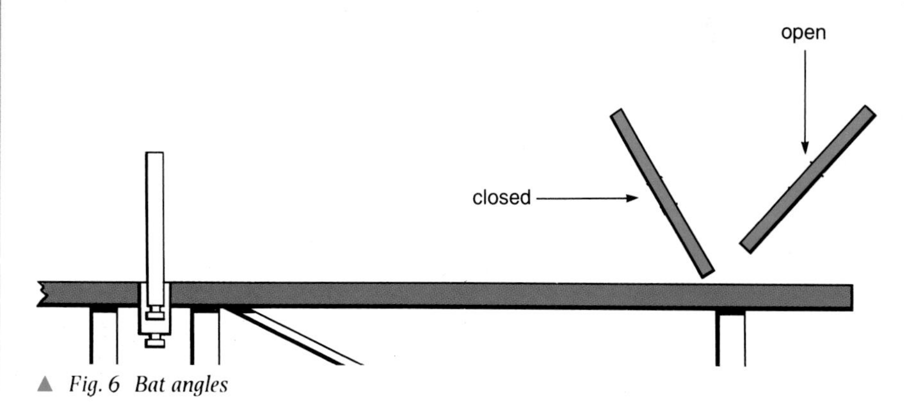

▲ *Fig. 6 Bat angles*

The basic strokes

There are four basic strokes from which all advanced techniques are developed:

- the backhand push
- the forehand drive
- the backhand drive
- the forehand push.

(The order in which these strokes are learnt depends on the 'feeder'. The backhand push is easier for two novices to gain quick success and enjoy playing rallies. The forehand drive needs a steady 'feed' to learn the stroke in the first instance.)

Backhand push

From the ready position, the ball is hit with an open bat angle imparting slight backspin on the ball. The body action is limited as the ball is played in front of the body with the player taking a square stance. The stroke is short with movement coming from the elbow and with a short follow through towards the bottom of the net. The free arm helps the player to maintain balance.

This stroke is commonly used to return short balls and backspin services.

The backhand push may be used to return ▶ backspun services and to vary the length of backspin shots, making it difficult for the opponent to attack

The bat angle is open and so backspin is ▶ imparted to the ball

▲ *The backhand push is technically the easiest of the basic strokes*

▲ *Often it is the first stroke that is taught because it is relatively easy for two beginners to play rallies*

Forehand drive

This is probably the most exciting stroke. From the ready position, the body turns to the right so that the ball is hit from a side-to-square stance. The bat angle is closed and the player imparts topspin on the ball by using a 'saluting' action. The stroke is of medium length with the ball being hit at the top of the bounce. The free arm assists with balance and body rotation.

This stroke is used to return any long balls and to hit any high balls with the aim of winning the point quickly. In order to hit a high ball, the player needs to use a longer stroke – this is known as a 'smash' or a 'kill'. When the forehand drive is played with a very short stroke and the ball is hit before the peak of its bounce, the stroke is called a 'block'.

Attacking players try to play their forehand drives in order to dominate the table ▶

▲ *Good footwork is essential so that this stroke may be played from the backhand corner of the table*

▲ *The forehand drive is the first of the attacking strokes to be learned and it is often considered the most exciting*

▲ *Topspin is imparted to the ball by using a down-to-up action of the arm with the bat having a 'closed' angle*

▲ *All high balls are punished by playing a 'smash' or 'kill', the aim being to win the point outright*

▲ *The bat angle must remain closed in order to bring the ball downwards. Weight is transferred from the right to the left foot as the ball is struck*

Backhand drive

This is similar in technique to the backhand push except that the bat angle is closed so that topspin can be imparted by the bat arm moving in a down-to-up direction. The follow through finishes with the bat pointing towards the top of the net.

This stroke is used to counteract topspun balls and to return topspun serves.

Top right *The backhand drive is played with a closed bat angle and the stroke is finished with the bat pointing towards the top of the net*

The backhand drive is used to return ▶ *topspun balls or to attack pushed balls. It is an attacking stroke.*

Forehand push

Technically the most difficult of the basic strokes, the forehand push is used to play short, low balls and to return backspun serves. From the ready position, the player plays a short stroke with an open bat angle, imparting slight backspin on the ball. The body position is side-to-square to the line of the ball. The player is close to the table with the bat arm moving from the elbow. The free arm again assists with balance and body rotation.

▲ *Good touch play with the push strokes is essential to vary the placement of the ball*

▲ *The forehand push may be used to play any short balls that cannot be attacked*

▲ *The forehand push is technically the hardest of the basic strokes and, as a consequence, is usually the last to be taught*

The forehand push is played with an open blade with the aim of imparting slight backspin to the ball. The stroke finishes with the bat pointing towards the bottom of the net ▶

Service

The service is undoubtedly the most important stroke in table tennis. If you can't serve then you can't win. However, in the early learning stages a player should concentrate on two factors:

- the length of the service
- the type of spin.

Topspin and backspin serves can be learnt easily from the same techniques that are used to play the four basic strokes. If a player then focuses on positioning these serves – both long and short – then the variations are immense.

The forehand serve from the backhand corner of the table ▶

The service law states:

At the start of service the ball shall be stationary, resting freely on the flat, open palm of the server's free hand, behind the end line and above the level of the playing surface.

The server shall then project the ball near vertically upwards, without imparting spin, so that it rises at least 16 cm [6 in] after leaving the palm of the free hand.

As the ball is falling from the highest point of its trajectory, the server shall strike it so that it touches first his court and then, after passing over or around the net, the receiver's court; in doubles, the ball shall touch successively the right-hand court of server and receiver.

The ball and racket shall be above the level of the playing surface from the last moment at which the ball is stationary before being projected until it is struck.

When the ball is struck it shall be behind the server's end line but not further back than the part of the server's body, other than his arm, head or leg, which is furthest from his end line.

The service begins when the ball and the bat are held above the height of the table, and the ball is in play the moment it leaves the hand. A poor throw or a miss with the bat is a lost point.

A good service must bounce on both sides of the table. In singles, the ball may bounce anywhere but in doubles it must bounce diagonally from the right-hand side.

If a service ball touches the net, but is otherwise correct, the umpire calls a 'let' and the service is taken again.

The choice of service is decided by the toss of a coin. The winner of the toss may choose:

- to serve
- to receive the service
- which end to start playing from.

If he chooses either of the first two options, his opponent may choose the third and vice versa.

Service return

The player who is receiving the service should be in the ready position, so that he can move easily in any direction to cover all possible angles that the server may use. The stroke used to return service depends on the type of serve, but generally speaking forehand and backhand drives are used to return topspin and long serves, whereas forehand and backhand pushes are used for short serves with backspin.

After the ball has been correctly served, play continues until one player fails to make a good return and so loses the point.

A good return is when the ball bounces once only on the receiver's half of the table. It must then be hit (a 'hit' includes the hand holding the bat) and returned to the opponent's side of the table without touching any obstacle (other than the net). There is no height limit to the path of the ball. It may pass above the lights but it must not touch them. If the ball touches any obstacle the ball is 'dead' and the last striker loses the point.

A good return can pass over the net at any point in its length, or around the side of the net post. It is also a good return if the ball passes under the net post.

A player is allowed to follow a spinning ball back across the net and strike it over the opponent's half of the table as long as he does not touch the net or net posts with his bat or clothing.

Scoring

In table tennis the scoring system is very simple. Either player may score a point regardless of whether or not he is serving.

A point is scored if:

- the opponent fails to make a good return
- the opponent moves the table
- the opponent touches the table, net or net post with his free hand
- the opponent volleys the ball over the table or in front of an imaginary extension of the base line (i.e. at the side of the table)
- the opponent fails to serve legally.

Net cord balls have to be played in the same way, except in service as already mentioned.

Service changes every five points.

A game is played to 21 points unless both players have scored 20 points. In this case play continues, with alternate serves until one player wins by two clear points, e.g. 23–21.

A match is usually the best of three games, although in some competitions the best of five games is played. There have been experiments with different types of scoring, notably an 11-up system. Each competition states the regulations for the event.

In **doubles**, the players must hit the ball alternately and in strict rotation. This means that in any one game a player always hits the ball to the same opponent and receives from the opponent's partner.

In every game the serving pair may start with either player. In the first game, the receiving players may choose which player receives the service first. After the first game, the receiving sequence must be reversed game by game and again in any deciding game when one pair have scored ten points.

Doubles: ready to serve ▶

The service in doubles must be made from the right-hand half of the table, marked by a 0.317 cm ($\frac{1}{8}$ in) line down the centre of the table. A bounce on the line counts as a good service.

After serving his five points, the player moves to allow his partner to receive the next five services and then to serve for five points.

So, in a game of players A and B versus players X and Y, the sequence will be as follows:

- 1st five points – A serves to X
- 2nd five points – X serves to B
- 3rd five points – B serves to Y
- 4th five points – Y serves to A.

This sequence is then repeated until the game is won or until a score of 20-all is reached. At 20-all, the sequence is maintained but each player serves and receives only one point (instead of a series of five).

The expedite system

The expedite system is the method provided to prevent unduly long games. It is introduced after 15 minutes of play (or at any time earlier if both players or pairs agree). Once the system has been introduced, it remains in force for the remainder of the match.

Under this system, the players serve only one service each and the server has 12 strokes after his service to win the point. If his service and the 12 subsequent strokes are safely returned by the receiver, then the receiver wins the point. The game is won in the normal way by a player winning 21 points, or after 20-all by two clear points.

The expedite system was introduced, like the tie-break in tennis, to encourage the server to attack and so maintain exciting play.

Warm-up

Before taking part in any physical activity, players should spend at least a few minutes warming up. Warming up helps to warm the muscles and so prevent injury; it also mobilises the joints and raises the heart rate. In short, warm-ups help a player to perform to his best.

The warm-up should start with general body exercises such as light jogging or skipping which should be slowly increased in intensity. These should be followed by static stretching exercises covering the whole body, beginning at the top and working down as follows:

- neck and shoulders (do not roll the neck in a full circle as this may cause damage to the vertebrae)
- arms and chest
- lower back and stomach
- groin and hips
- upper leg
- knees
- lower leg and ankle.

Ballistic stretching exercises which involve bouncing or jerking movements could cause injury and so should be avoided.

The warm-up should take place just prior to the beginning of the practice session or match.

Cool down

Cool downs after exercise will help to avoid any stiffness or soreness in the muscles. Slow jogging or walking and light stretching are ideal and should be continued for a few minutes until the body returns to a near resting state.

Practice

People play table tennis for different reasons – to socialise, for exercise, for competition or just for fun. Undoubtedly, winning is more enjoyable than losing. To be successful at table tennis, as in every other sport, the player must commit time to practice.

Practice can be divided into two elements:

- practice to improve the strokes, i.e. technical practice
- practice to improve the tactics, i.e. tactical practice.

Technical practice

Stroke practice is either **regular** or **irregular**.

Regular practices involve situations in which the player knows where the ball is going to be placed. This allows the player to concentrate on improving techniques. *See* fig. 7.

Irregular practices involve an element of surprise when the player does not know where the ball is going. *See* fig. 8. These practices are harder because the player has to look for clues from the opponent and learn to anticipate when the ball is likely to be hit in a different direction.

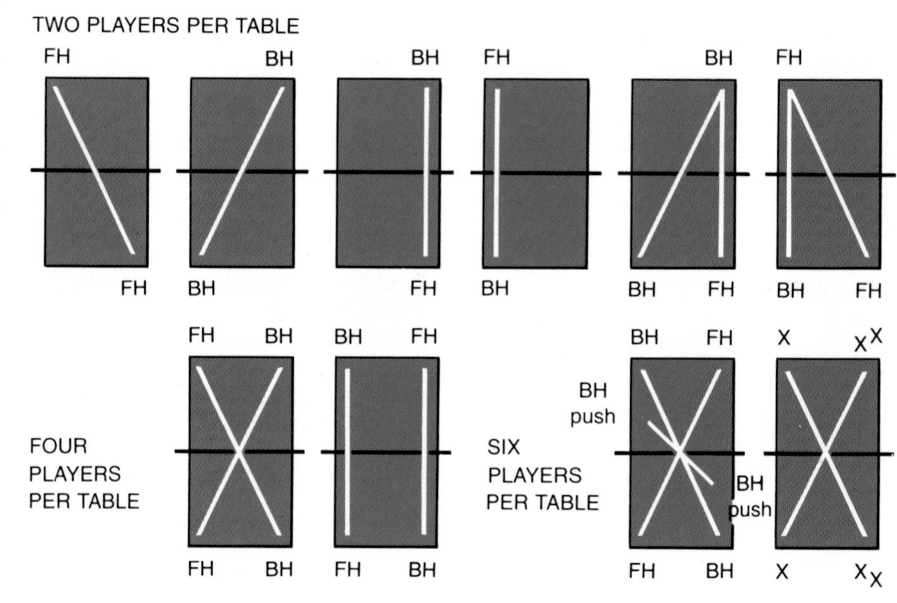

Fig. 7 Technical practice: regular practices

Tactical practice

Tactical practices are very individual since the tactics that each player uses will depend on his style of play and his technical abilities.

For example, a player with a strong forehand drive may practise fast top-spin services followed by forehand drives, aiming to win the point on the third ball. *See* fig. 9.

A player with a preference for back-hand strokes may find that short back-spin services to the backhand side may result in greater opportunity to play a backhand on the third ball. *See* fig. 10.

Tactical practices should be devised to allow a player to play to his strengths while exploiting the oppo-nent's weaknesses (if known).

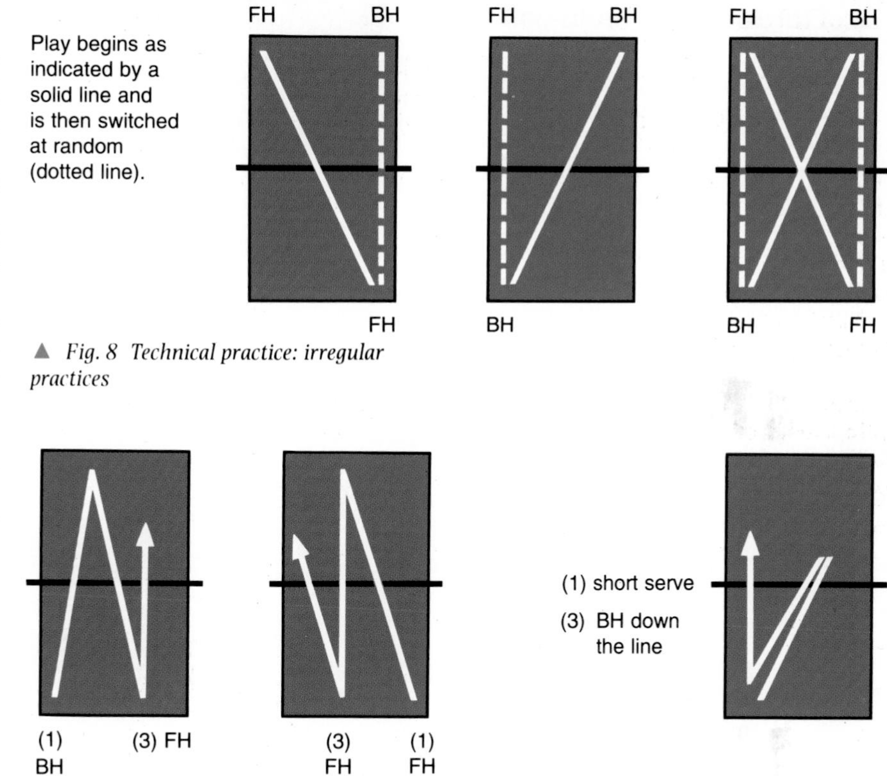

▲ *Fig. 8 Technical practice: irregular practices*

Fig. 9 Tactical practice ▶

▲ *Fig. 10 Tactical practice*

Use of the robot and multi-ball

Practices may include the use of a 'robot'. This is a machine that shoots balls out at varying speeds and with different spins. If used properly, robots are useful aids for improving stroke production and for a single player if he does not have an available partner.

Multi-ball practice is also popular. This is when a coach 'feeds' a number of balls in quick succession to a player. This is better than using a 'robot' because the feeder can vary the spin, speed and positioning of the ball to offer a more realistic practice. This type of practice is physically very demanding.

The ETTA Skills Award Scheme lists more practices that are suitable for players of all different standards.

▲ *Practising with a 'robot'*

Multi-ball practice ▶

Fun games

Table tennis is fun and there are numerous variations of the main game that can be used to maintain the enjoyment while retaining a competitive element.

Overtaking

The players balance the ball on their bats and run around the outside of the playing area. Anyone who is overtaken or who drops the ball is out.

This can be advanced with players bouncing the ball on their bat – either forehand, backhand or alternating forehand and backhand.

Minute rallies

Two players play a rally and count the number of strokes played in one minute.

A variation is to count the number of strokes played without a mistake.

Round the table

All players are at one end of the table with a feeder at the other end. After hitting the ball, each player must run around the table to rejoin the line.

A variation is to have equal numbers at each end of the table and the players run to the opposite end after hitting the ball. Players have three lives, one of which is forfeited on each mistake.

Team singles

One player from each team plays a point. The losing player is replaced by the next member of his team for the second point. A player winning three points in a row must retire.

▼ *Round the table*

Targets

- A small target (e.g. a postcard) is placed on the table. Two players play a rally on one diagonal (where the target is) and score points as normal. If they hit the target they score two points.
- A target (e.g. an A3 sheet of paper) is placed on either side of the net. Each player serves alternately, aiming to hit the target. When the target has been hit three times, the paper is folded in half. Each player aims to make his target smaller than his opponent's.
- In teams, players serve to various targets of differing sizes, scoring points if they are successful. Points may be allocated according to difficulty (size, position).

Cricket

Each team has a minimum of three players. One team bats and the other fields. One of the fielding team throws the ball underarm over the net (at head height) to bounce on the opposite side of the table. The batsman hits the ball so that it lands on the opposite side of the table and then on the floor before the fielders can catch him out. If successful he scores a run and continues his innings. He remains in until: he misses the ball; he hits the ball into the net; he misses the table; or he is caught out. When all players on the batting side have had an innings, the teams change over.

Cricket ▶

Relays

In teams, the first player runs to the table and serves the ball. He then runs around the table and catches the ball after it has bounced once and before it hits the floor. If successful, he scores one point and he runs to give the ball to the next player in his team. The first team to score ten points wins. The service should be legal.

A variation is to catch the ball after two bounces or to serve to a specific target.

Advanced techniques

The block

The block is a variation of the forehand and backhand drive which is used to counteract topspin. The ball is struck very early (before the peak of the bounce) with very little follow through of the bat, and so reduces the time that the opponent has to recover between strokes.

The forehand block is a very short stroke, ▶ played with a closed bat angle. It is used to counteract topspin strokes

▲ *The backhand block is used to counteract topspun balls and to return topspun serves. The ball is hit with a closed angle*

◄ *When the ball is hit before the peak of the bounce, as in the backhand block, the opponent is put under pressure since the ball is returned very quickly*

The loop

The loop is an advanced stroke in which accentuated topspin is imparted on the ball. It may be played on both the forehand and backhand. To play a successful loop, the player must accentuate his body movement by pushing strongly from the legs, using a longer stroke, and accelerating the bat arm, making light but fast contact on the ball.

▼ *The forehand loop imparts accentuated topspin on the ball by the light but fast brushing action of the bat on the ball. Good use of the legs is essential if power is to be produced*

A good wrist action is vital to an effective execution of the backhand loop

The chop

The chop is an advanced stroke in which accentuated backspin is imparted on the ball. It may be played on both the forehand and backhand. The chop is a development of the push strokes and is used to return topspin strokes when the player is away from the table. The chop differs from the push in that the stroke is longer, the ball is hit at or after the peak of the bounce, and there is greater body action.

The forehand chop is a defensive stroke in ▶ which accentuated backspin is imparted to the ball by an up-to-down action of the bat. The bat strikes the ball with an open blade and the follow through continues downwards towards the floor

▲ *The backhand chop. Note the path of the bat, from shoulder height down to the floor, while maintaining good balance*

The advanced service

Advanced players tend to use a forehand service from the backhand corner of the table. This allows them to play the next stroke with their forehand, which for most players is their strongest stroke. However, the player must have fast footwork for this to be profitable because the whole table has to be covered.

Players usually alter their grip for this service. A very loose grip is required so that a fast wrist action can be used to produce maximum spin.

▲ *This player uses his combination bat (i.e. different types of rubber on each side of the blade) to produce very different kinds of spin*

The service begins with the ball resting on the palm of the hand, which is held above the table. The ball is thrown upwards and struck when it is descending

Another high toss service. Note the loose grip which allows for maximum wrist action and therefore increased spin

Other advanced techniques

Top players use other variations of the strokes already described. These include topspins with early, peak and late bounce contact points; chop strokes with spin variations such as heavy backspin or float; drop shots and chop blocks. The full explanation of these strokes does not come within the remit of this book. Further information should be obtained from the ETTA's Coaching Manual.

A backhand sidespin serve ▶

Programme planning

To be successful at table tennis, it is essential that your training programme is well organised and carefully planned. A single session may be organised as follows:

- warm-up .... 10 minutes
- knock-up .... 5 minutes
- regular exercises .... 45 minutes
- irregular exercises ...... 25 minutes
- conditional play .... 15 minutes
- match play .... 15 minutes
- cool down................... 5 minutes.

When more than one session is planned, a physical training programme should be incorporated. This should include work on stamina, speed, flexibility and strength.

Physical training is an important part of programme planning. The intensity of the physical training will depend on the age and the standard of the players. Obviously, casual players will not be interested in physical training, but those whose aspirations are higher will understand the need for total fitness.

Physical training can be performed on or off the table. Multi-ball drills are ideal for on-table exercises, as are shadow play exercises.

Most stamina and flexibility work is practised off the table. This includes distance running, skipping and a variety of stretching exercises.

The serious competitor needs to make long-term plans. This is called 'periodisation'. The aim is to train so that the player can 'peak' for important competitons.

A periodised yearly cycle for juniors would include three phases:

- preparation
- competiton
- rest.

The preparation phase would be from July to early September. This time is used to concentrate on improving technique and tactical awareness.

The competition phase runs from September to the end of May. This is when players are competing in various competitions and trying to gain the best possible results.

The rest phase is in June when competitions have finished. This is not an inactive time but it is a time when players participate in other sports to maintain their fitness without getting stale by playing too much table tennis.

The timings of these phases will vary depending on the level of play. For example, The European Youth Championships take place in July and this would be included in the competition phase.

Coaching

The ETTA, in conjunction with Dunlop, have produced a Skills Award Scheme which has five different grades. This offers a differentiated programme of practices which are suitable for all levels of players.

Players who wish to improve their playing standards will need to have some coaching. Many schools run table tennis clubs where there is a member of staff who has some expertise. However, for a player to proceed further up the ladder of success, he will need to join a club. Lists of local clubs can be found in the libraries or by contacting the national governing body.

Once in a club, players will be able to progress through the Coaching Scheme. If they reach national potential, they will be able to attend Centres for Excellence before hopefully playing for their country.

**RULES FOR
ROOKIE AWARD**

**If you pass this you can be proud
of being a good beginner**

SKILLS TESTS DEVISED BY ENGLISH TABLE TENNIS ASSOCIATION
AND ENGLISH SCHOOLS TABLE TENNIS ASSOCIATION

Note: The following abbreviations are used to denote specific areas on the table. (See diagram)
B = Backhand area
F = Forehand area
BA = Backhand Target area
FA = Forehand Target area
A sheet of A3 paper (or 2 pieces of A4) is ideal for indicating size of the target area and can be moved to suit the test.

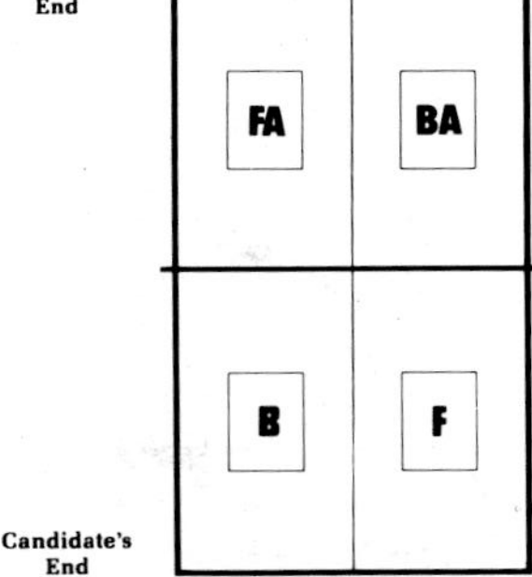

Test 1: Objective – to improve "feel" of ba: and ball
(No table is needed for this test).
Demonstrate forehand tap bounce.
Pass: 5 bounces with maximum one error.
(3 attempts allowed).

Test 2: Objective – to improve "feel" of bat and ball
As test 1, played with backhand.

Test 3: Objective – to improve stance and alertness
(Any table may be used for this test).
Demonstrate a good "ready" position; slightly crouched, knees slightly bent. Feet apart, more than shoulder width. Bat held lightly, pointing at and ready to track an imaginary on-coming ball.

Test 4: Objective – to improve skill in guiding (not "hitting") the ball
Candidate drops ball from a height of 25cm at position B. After it has bounced, candidate steers it backhand to area BA. Controller catches and returns the ball.
Pass: 10 balls with maximum 2 errors.
(3 attempts allowed).

Test 5: Objective – to improve skill in guiding (not "hitting") the ball
Exactly as Test 4 but dropping the ball at position F and steering it forehand to area FA.

Test 6: Objective – to improve mobility
(Any table of suitable width may be used for this test).
Demonstrate 6 movements to either side, positions F to B, with bat but without ball.
Pass: Use of small skip-steps, with weight towards the toes and never closing feet together.

Test 7: Objective – to start a rally
Candidate must make 3 consecutive good services with either backhand or forehand (3 attempts allowed).

Test 8: Objective – to play a short rally
Candidate must play 5 consecutive backhand pushes on the diagonal (3 attempts allowed).

Test 9: Objective – to play a short rally
Candidate mus: play 5 consecutive forehand drives on the diagonal (3 attempts allowed).

This completes the Rookie Award. Assessors should now complete the Awards Form recording the names of the successful Candidates and send it to the
Awards Administrator, English Table Tennis Association, Queensbury House, Havelock Road, Hastings, East Sussex TN34 1HF. Tel: 0424 722525

RULES FOR IMPROVERS AWARD

If you pass this, you are making steady progress, and should go straight on to try the PLAYER Award.

SKILLS TESTS DEVISED BY ENGLISH TABLE TENNIS ASSOCIATION AND ENGLISH SCHOOLS TABLE TENNIS ASSOCIATION

Note: The following abbreviations will be used to denote specific areas on the table. (See diagram)
B = Backhand area
F = Forehand area
A sheet of A3 paper (or 2 pieces of A4) is ideal for indicating size of the target area and can be moved to suit the test.

Controller's End

C2 | C1

B | F

m

Candidate's End

Test 1: All backhand push control (From 2 points, returning to 1 Target)
Using sound footwork, return 30 slow push shots alternately, from B and M. to C1.
Pass: 30 successes 4th error fails.

Test 2: All forehand controlled drives (For attacking style Candidates)
Play 30 forehand Drives alternately from F and M. to C2.
Pass: 30 successes 4th error fails.

Test 2a: All forehand push control (For defensive style Candidates)
Against forehand Push, play 30 forehand Push shots alternately from F and M to C1.
Pass: 30 successes 4th error fails.

Test 3: All backhand controlled drive
Using sound footwork play 30 backhand controlled Drives alternately from B and M to C1.
Pass: 30 successes 4th error fails.

Test 4: Combined block returns
Against controlled Drives, play 30 backhand and forehand Block returns alternately, from B and F to C2.
Pass: 30 successes 4th error fails.

Test 5: Long drive services
(1) From the correct position, serve with forehand, ball to land beyond C2.

(2) As (1) but serve with backhand, ball to land beyond C1.
Pass: In each case, 5 successes within 8 attempts.

Test 6: Short-touch services
(1) From the correct position behind the baseline serve short forehand services so as to clear the net and bounce twice on the table.

(2) As (1) but serve with backhand.
Pass: In each case, 5 successes to be achieved within 8 attempts.

This completes the Improvers Award. Assessors should now complete the Awards Form recording the names of the successful Candidates and send it to the Awards Administrator, English Table Tennis Association, Queensbury House, Havelock Road, Hastings, East Sussex TN34 1HF. Tel: 0424 722525

RULES FOR PLAYER AWARD

If you pass this you have the shots to play matches. Why not have a go in your local league in one of the lower divisions?

SKILLS TESTS DEVISED BY ENGLISH TABLE TENNIS ASSOCIATION AND ENGLISH SCHOOLS TABLE TENNIS ASSOCIATION

Note: The following abbreviations are used to denote specific areas on the table. (See diagram)

B = Backhand area
F = Forehand area
BA = Backhand Target area
FA = Forehand Target area

A sheet of A3 paper (or 2 pieces of A4) is ideal for indicating size of the target area and can be moved to suit the test.

Controller's End

FA BA

B F

Candidate's End

Test 1: Return of varied services
Required: Return by suitable push or attack, services which have been delivered with medium strength sidespins, including elements of topspin and backspin.
Pass: 16 successes 5th error fails.

Test 2: Services variation
Deliver services of varying strength, incorporating sidespin, alternating left and right.
Pass: 16 successes 5th error fails.

Test 3: Combining forehand top spin drive and forehand push
Return 30 balls, which have been alternately pushed and backspun, by using respectively topspin drive and short push-shots, played alternately, on the diagonal line from F to FA.
Pass: 30 correct 5th error fails.

Test 4: Combining backhand drive and backhand push
As Test 3 but using backhand throughout, from B to BA.
Pass: 30 correct 5th error fails.

Test 5: Combining forehand block **returns with forehand push**
Return 30 balls which have been alternately driven and pushed, on the same line, by using, respectively block returns and short pushes, played alternately on the same line, F to FA.

Test 6: Combining backhand block returns with backhand push.
As Test 5 but using backhand throughout, B to BA.
Pass: 30 correct 5th error fails.

Test 7: Maintaining attack against switched drives from the Controller
Maintain 10 triple sequences as follows:
2 forehand Topspin Drives, plus 1 backhand Topspin Drive from F and B to FA.
Pass: 10 good sequences 5th error fails

Test 8: As Test 7 but
Sequences of 2 backhand Topspin Drives, plus 1 forehand Topspin Drive, from B and F, to BA.
Pass: 10 good sequences 5th error fails.

Test 9: Laws and Rules
Answer 10 "everyday" questions on Laws and match procedure. Points allowed: For complete answer 3; for correct "sense" 2; for a part answer 1.
Pass: Score 22 out of 30.

This completes the Player award. Assessors should now complete the Awards Form recording the names of the successful Candidates and send it to the

Awards Administrator, English Table Tennis Association, Queensbury House, Havelock Road, Hastings, East Sussex TN34 1HF. Tel: 0424 722525

RULES FOR MATCHPLAYER AWARD

If you pass this award you ought to think of trying one or two small tournaments

SKILLS TESTS DEVISED BY ENGLISH TABLE TENNIS ASSOCIATION AND ENGLISH SCHOOLS TABLE TENNIS ASSOCIATION

Controller's End

G H

J K

Candidate's End

Test 1: Forehand drives – close and distant
Return 30 drives by means of forehand drives in sequences of 2 as follows: 2 "close", 2 "distant" 2 "close", etc. All returns played from K to G.
Pass: 30 correct 3rd error fails.

Test 2: Backhand drives – close and distant
As Test 1 but using backhand drive. All returns played from J to H.
Pass: 30 correct 3rd error fails.

Test 3: 3rd ball attack
Deliver 10 short backhand services which are to be flicked or pushed long alternately to K and J. The Candidate must follow up with a suitable 3rd ball attack.
Pass: 10 correct 4th error fails.

Test 4: As test 3 but with forehand services
Pass: 10 correct 4th error fails.

Test 5: Combining forehand backspin returns with forehand push
Return 30 balls which have been alternately driven and pushed, on the same line, by using respectively forehand backspin returns, and forehand short pushes, played alternately.
Pass: 30 correct 5th error fails.

Test 6: Combining backhand backspin returns with backhand push
As Test 5.
Pass: 30 correct 5th error fails.

Test 7: Effective receive of short service – forehand and backhand
Return short service to forehand or backhand with appropriate selection of stroke using short push or long fast push against backspin service, and flick against the float service (i.e. service with no spin).
Against 20 varied serves, the Candidate must make at least 12 successful returns (4 of each type).

Test 8: Scoring a match
The Candidate must demonstrate the ability to score a match (practical test).

This completes the Matchplayer Award. Assessors should now complete the Awards Form recording the names of successful Candidates and send it to the Awards Administrator, English Table Tennis Association, Queensbury House, Havelock Road, Hastings, East Sussex TN34 1HF. Tel: 0424 722525

Assessors for the Matchplayer Award should be a qualified ETTA coach to at least Assistant Coach level.

SKILLS TESTS DEVISED BY ENGLISH TABLE TENNIS ASSOCIATION AND ENGLISH SCHOOLS TABLE TENNIS ASSOCIATION

Controller's End

G		H
	L	
	E	
	m	
B		
J	F	K

Candidate's End

Test 1: Forehand and backhand Topspin drive under pressure
Play 30 alternate topspin drives, backhand from B to H, and forehand from F to H against fast block returns. Good position and footwork required throughout.
Pass: 30 correct 3rd error fails.

Test 2: Service and service laws
Explain by action the main points of a legal service together with the important features of an effective service. Demonstrate a legal high toss forehand service with recovery and follow-up shot.

Test 3: Combining forehand and backhand topspin drives
Against slow backspin returns, which have been placed at random, play 20 forehand and backhand topspin drives to H and G. Controller to ensure reasonable distribution to both forehand and backhand.
Pass: 20 correct 3rd error fails.

Test 4: Combining forehand and backhand defensive backspin returns
Against drives which have been placed at random, play 20 forehand and backhand backspin returns to L. Controllor to ensure reasonable distribution to both forehand and backhand.
Pass: 20 correct 3rd error fails.

Test 5: Topspin attack distribution with dropshots
Play 10 triple sequences as follows: Dropshot to E. Backhand drive to H.
Forehand drive G, and then repeat. Controllor returns all balls to area M with backspin. Candidate may keep the ball in play with simple placing shots between the actual sequences.
Pass: 10 triple sequences 4th error fails.

Test 6: Display understanding of varied forehand topspin
Play 8 double sequences as follows: slow topspin against backspin returns followed by fast topspin against blocked returns. Sequence must be according to opportunity, a continuous rally is not demanded.
Pass: 8 double sequences 3rd error fails.

Test 7: Display understanding of varied backhand topspin
As test 6 but with backhand
Pass: 8 double sequences, 3rd error fail.

Test 8: Triple sequences
Play 10 triple sequences of forehand and backhand topspin all from blocked returns. Backhand from J and forehand from F and K all to L.
Pass: 10 triple sequences 4th error fails.

Test 9: Defensive lob to smash
Play several lobs against smash to a height of at least 2m above the table.

Test 10: Smash against defensive lob
The reverse of Test 8.

This completes the Masters Award. Assessors should now complete the Awards Form recording the names of successful Candidates and send it to the Awards Administrator, English Table Tennis Association, Queensbury House, Havelock Road, Hastings, East Sussex TN34 1HF. Tel: 0424 722525

Notes:
(1) Assessors for the Masters Award should be a qualified ETTA coach at least to Coach level.

(2) The Candidate must pass seven tests of his/her own selection from the ten available.

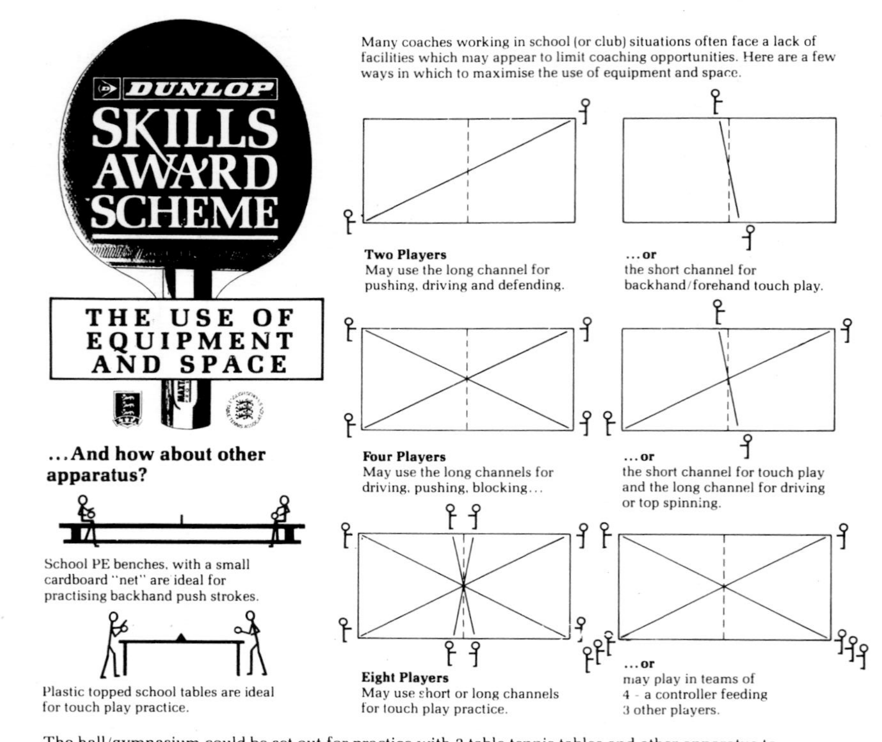

THE USE OF EQUIPMENT AND SPACE

Many coaches working in school (or club) situations often face a lack of facilities which may appear to limit coaching opportunities. Here are a few ways in which to maximise the use of equipment and space.

Two Players
May use the long channel for pushing, driving and defending.

...or
the short channel for backhand/forehand touch play.

Four Players
May use the long channels for driving, pushing, blocking...

...or
the short channel for touch play and the long channel for driving or top spinning.

Eight Players
May use short or long channels for touch play practice.

...or
may play in teams of 4 - a controller feeding 3 other players.

...And how about other apparatus?

School PE benches, with a small cardboard "net" are ideal for practising backhand push strokes.

Plastic topped school tables are ideal for touch play practice.

The hall/gymnasium could be set out for practice with 3 table tennis tables and other apparatus to incorporate 16 players who move around this circuit.

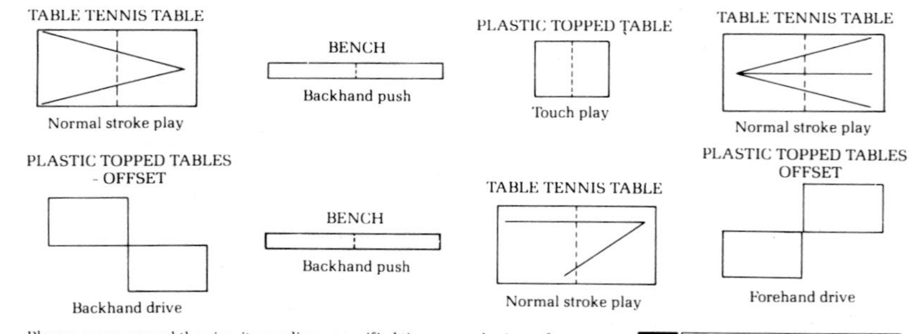

Players move around the circuit spending a specified time on each piece of equipment. Partners may be changed and the circuit repeated as necessary. These are just a few basic tips. These principles can be extended to maximise the use of the equipment available and give the Dunlop Skills Award Scheme a much broader application.

Competitive play

The newcomer to table tennis probably began by playing at school, in a youth club or at a local table tennis club. As progress is made, competitive play is necessary. The English Schools Table Tennis Association (ESTTA) runs both individual and team competitions for both boys and girls. These are open to any player who attends an affiliated school.

The English Table Tennis Association (ETTA) is responsible for co-ordinating a programme of tournaments throughout the country for cadet (under 14 years), junior (under 17 years), senior (over 17 years) and veteran (over 40 years) players. These tournaments include singles and doubles events, and age group and ability banded competitions.

There are also British League competitions for junior, senior and veteran players.

In addition to these 'open' events, there are a large number of 'closed' tournaments. These all have some restrictions. For example a 'Country Closed' is only for players who live in a particular area.

All of these provide valuable match experience and will help a talented player to be noticed by the selectors and perhaps be invited to join county, regional or national squad training camps.

Affiliation

An affiliated player is one who attaches himself to the national association, either directly or through membership of a club or affiliated organisation.

National governing bodies include:

The English Table Tennis Association
(Address on page 2.)

The English Schools Table Tennis Association
36 Froom Street
Chorley
Lancashire
PR6 0AN

The British Table Tennis Association for People with Disabilities
109 Stanbridge Road
Haddenham
Buckinghamshire
HP17 8HN

The Irish Table Tennis Association
46 Lorcan Villas
Santry
Dublin

The Scottish Table Tennis Association
Caledonia House
South Gyle
Edinburgh
EH12 9DQ

The Table Tennis Association of Wales
31 Maes y Celyn
Griffithstown
Pontypool
Gwent
NP4 5DG

Index